Linux Essentials for Cybersecurity Lab Manual

William "Bo" Rothwell

PEARSON IT CERTIFICATION

Linux Essentials for Cybersecurity Lab Manual

Copyright © 2019 by Pearson Education, Inc.

ISBN-13: 978-0-7897-6055-5
ISBN-10: 0-7897-6055-X

Library of Congress Control Number: 2018949197

01   18

Trademarks

All terms mentioned in this book that are known to be trademarks or service marks have been appropriately capitalized. Pearson IT Certification cannot attest to the accuracy of this information. Use of a term in this book should not be regarded as affecting the validity of any trademark or service mark.

Warning and Disclaimer

Every effort has been made to make this book as complete and as accurate as possible, but no warranty or fitness is implied. The information provided is on an "as is" basis. The author and the publisher shall have neither liability nor responsibility to any person or entity with respect to any loss or damages arising from the information contained in this book.

Special Sales

For information about buying this title in bulk quantities, or for special sales opportunities (which may include electronic versions; custom cover designs; and content particular to your business, training goals, marketing focus, or branding interests), please contact our corporate sales department at corpsales@pearsoned.com or (800) 382-3419.

For government sales inquiries, please contact governmentsales@pearsoned.com.

For questions about sales outside the U.S., please contact intlcs@pearson.com.

Editor-in-Chief
Mark Taub

Product Line Manager
Brett Bartow

Acquisitions Editor
Mary Beth Ray

Development Editor
Ellie Bru

Managing Editor
Sandra Schroeder

Project Editor
Mandie Frank

Copy Editor
Kitty Wilson

Proofreader
Debbie Williams

Technical Editor
Denise Kinsey

Publishing Coordinator
Vanessa Evans

Designer
Chuti Prasertsith

Compositor
Bronkella Publishing

Contents at a Glance

Table of Contents

About the Author

At the impressionable age of 14, **William "Bo" Rothwell** crossed paths with a TRS-80 Micro Computer System (affectionately known as a "Trash 80"). Soon after the adults responsible for Bo made the mistake of leaving him alone with the TRS-80, he immediately dismantled it and held his first computer class, showing his friends what made this "computer thing" work.

Since that experience, Bo's passion for understanding how computers work and sharing this knowledge with others has resulted in a rewarding career in IT training. His experience includes Linux, Unix, and programming languages such as Perl, Python, Tcl, and BASH. He is the founder and president of One Course Source, an IT training organization.

Dedication

For the last three books, I have thanked my wife and daughter for their patience and my
parents for all that they have done throughout my life. My gratitude continues, as always.
—William "Bo" Rothwell
May 2018

Acknowledgments

Thanks to everyone who has put in a direct effort toward making this book a success: You have my thanks, as always.

—William "Bo" Rothwell

May 2018

About the Technical Reviewer

Denise Kinsey, Ph.D., CISSP, CISCO, served as a Unix administrator (HP-UX) in the late 1990s and realized the power and flexibility of the operating system. This appreciation led to her home installation of different flavors of Linux and creation of several academic courses in Linux. With a strong background in cybersecurity, she works to share and implement best practices with her customers and students. Dr. Kinsey is an assistant professor at the University of Houston.

We Want to Hear from You!

As the reader of this book, *you* are our most important critic and commentator. We value your opinion and want to know what we're doing right, what we could do better, what areas you'd like to see us publish in, and any other words of wisdom you're willing to pass our way.

We welcome your comments. You can email or write to let us know what you did or didn't like about this book—as well as what we can do to make our books better.

Please note that we cannot help you with technical problems related to the topic of this book.

When you write, please be sure to include this book's title and author as well as your name and email address. We will carefully review your comments and share them with the author and editors who worked on the book.

Email: feedback@pearsonitcertification.com

Reader Services

Register your copy of *Linux Essentials for Cybersecurity Lab Manual* at www.pearsonitcertification.com for convenient access to downloads, updates, and corrections as they become available. To start the registration process, go to www.pearsonitcertification.com/register and log in or create an account*. Enter the product ISBN 9780789760555 and click Submit. When the process is complete, you will find any available bonus content under Registered Products.

*Be sure to check the box that you would like to hear from us to receive exclusive discounts on future editions of this product.

Figure Credits

Figure 1-1 Courtesy of CentOS Corporation

Figure 9-1 Courtesy of CentOS Corporation

Figure 10-1 Courtesy of CentOS Corporation

Figure 10-2 Courtesy of CentOS Corporation

Figure 11-1 Courtesy of CentOS Corporation

Figure 11-2 Courtesy of CentOS Corporation

Introduction

While developing *Linux Essentials for Cybersecurity*, it became clear that having hands-on experience would be very useful. Reading new content gets you only so far. To really become a Linux cybersecurity expert, you need practice. From that idea, this lab guide was born.

You will note that there are three different types of labs in this book:

- Labs in which you are presented with a short problem that requires only a single operation to complete.
- Labs that are more complex but in which we provide you with a guide to perform each step, one at a time.
- Scenario labs in which you are asked to solve a problem entirely on your own. These labs are designed to pose a greater challenge.

No matter the type, these labs are designed to be performed on live systems. While you could just write down the answers in some cases, I highly encourage you to work on Linux systems to complete all the labs. Not only will you get a sense of accomplishment, but the concepts and practices that are explored in *Linux Essentials for Cybersecurity* are more likely to find a permanent home in your brain.

Enjoy the journey and remember to always stand on the light side of the cybersecurity force.

Who Should Read This Book?

It might be easier to answer the question "Who shouldn't read this book?" Linux distributions are used by a large variety of individuals, including the following:

- Software developers
- Database administrators
- Website administrators
- Security administrators
- System administrators
- System recovery experts
- Big data engineers
- Hackers
- Government organizations
- Mobile users and developers (Android is a Linux distribution.)
- Chip vendors (Embedded Linux is found on many chip devices.)
- Digital forensic experts
- Educators

This isn't even a complete list! Linux is literally everywhere. It is the operating system used on Android phones. A large number of web and email servers run on Linux. Many network devices, such as routers and firewalls, have a version of embedded Linux installed on them.

This book is for people who want to better use Linux systems and ensure that the Linux systems they work on are as secure as possible.

How This Book Is Organized

Chapter 1, "Distributions and Key Components," includes labs in which you will install the Linux distributions that you will use throughout the rest of this book.

Chapter 2, "Working on the Command Line," covers labs related to the essential commands needed to work in the Linux environment.

Chapter 3, "Getting Help," provides you with hands-on experience to get additional information on Linux topics.

Chapter 4, "Editing Files," incorporates labs in which you practice using the **vim** editor.

Chapter 5, "When Things Go Wrong," provides you with experience in how to handle problems that may arise in Linux.

Chapter 6, "Managing Group Accounts," contains labs that focus on group accounts, including how to add, modify, and delete groups.

Chapter 7, "Managing User Accounts," contains labs that focus on user accounts, including how to add, modify, and delete users. This chapter also has a lab for securing user accounts as well as a lab for configuring **sudo**.

Chapter 8, "Develop an Account Security Policy," provides you with practice creating a user security policy and how to test the security of accounts.

Chapter 9, "File Permissions," focuses on securing files using Linux permissions. These labs also dive into more advanced topics, such as special permissions, **umask**, access control lists (ACLs), SELinux, and file attributes.

Chapter 10, "Manage Local Storage: Essentials," includes labs that are related to the concepts involved with local storage devices, such as how to create partitions and filesystems and some additional essential filesystem features.

Chapter 11, "Manage Local Storage: Advanced Features," provides hands-on activities related to advanced features of local storage devices, including how to create encrypted filesystems. You will get practice creating and managing logical volumes.

Chapter 12, "Manage Network Storage," provides exercises that are focused on making storage devices available across the network. Filesystem sharing techniques such as Network File System, Samba, and iSCSI are included.

Chapter 13, "Develop a Storage Security Policy," provides you with the experience of creating a security policy using the knowledge you acquired in Chapters 9–12. There is also a very important lab that covers performing filesystem backups.

Chapter 14, "Crontab and At," includes labs for managing the **crontab** and **at** systems.

Chapter 15, "Scripting," provides you with experience in shell scripting by having you create two shell scripts.

Chapter 16, "Common Automation Tasks," includes labs on creating shell scripts that are commonly used to automate tasks on Linux systems.

Chapter 17, "Develop an Automation Security Policy," provides you with the experience to create a security policy using the knowledge you acquired in Chapters 14–16. This chapter also includes a hands-on lab on securing the **crontab** and **at** systems.

Chapter 18, "Networking Basics," provides labs that help you explore network components on Linux.

Chapter 19, "Network Configuration," covers the process of configuring your system to connect to a network, both on Ubuntu and CentOS.

Chapter 20, "Network Service Configuration: Essential Services," includes labs for configuring several network-based tools, including DNS and email servers.

Chapter 21, "Network Service Configuration: Web Services," provides the experience of configuring several network-based tools, including the Apache web server and Squid.

Chapter 22, "Connecting to Remote Systems," includes labs on configuring LDAP, FTP, and SSH servers.

Chapter 23, "Develop a Network Security Policy," provides you with the experience to create a security policy using the knowledge you acquired in Chapters 18–22.

Chapter 24, "Process Control," includes labs on starting, viewing, and controlling processes (programs).

Chapter 25, "System Logging," gives you hands-on experience with viewing system logs as well as how to configure a system to create custom log entries.

Chapter 26, "Red Hat–Based Software Management," includes labs on administering software on Red Hat–based systems such as Fedora and CentOS.

Chapter 27, "Debian–Based Software Management," includes labs on administering software on Debian–based systems, such as Ubuntu.

Chapter 28, "System Booting," gives you practice configuring GRUB and managing the boot process.

Chapter 29, "Develop a Software Management Security Policy," provides you with the experience to create a security policy using the knowledge you acquired in Chapters 26–28. In addition, you will explore CVE reports.

Chapter 30, "Footprinting," includes labs that cover the techniques that hackers use to discover information about systems.

Chapter 31, "Firewalls," explores labs focused on configuring software that protects your systems from network-based attacks.

Chapter 32, "Intrusion Detection," provides you with experience using tools and techniques that help you determine if someone has successfully compromised the security of your systems.

Chapter 33, "Additional Security Tasks," includes labs that cover a variety of additional Linux security features, including the fail2ban service, VPNs, and file encryption.

Chapter 1

Distributions and Key Components

The goal of this lab is to help you install the three operating systems that you will use during the remainder of the labs. Oracle Virtual Box should be installed on your system before you proceed. You will also need at least 8GB of RAM (4GB for your host operating system and 4GB for the virtual machine). Note that while you will be installing three Linux distributions, only one will be "active" (booted up) at any given point during these labs.

You will also need 36GB total hard drive space for the three distributions (two distributions will use 10GB of space each, and the other will use 16GB of space).

Lab 1.1 Installing CentOS

STEP 1. Go to **https://wiki.centos.org/Download** and click the mirrors link for the ISO images:

STEP 2. Click on a mirror site of your choosing and then click on the **CentOS-7-x86_64-Everything-1708. iso** link to download the file. It takes some time for the file to download.

STEP 3. Start Oracle VirtualBox and then click the **New** button.

STEP 4. Enter **CENTOS 7 - for class** in the Name box.

STEP 5. Change the memory size to **4196 MB** and click the **Create** button.

STEP 6. Change the file size to **10.00 GB**.

STEP 7. Change the storage on physical hard disk to **Fixed Size** and click the **Create** button.

STEP 8. When you are returned to the main Oracle VirtualBox screen, click on the **Start** button.

STEP 9. Click on the small folder icon next to the drop-down list and navigate to the location where you downloaded the CentOS ISO file. Select that file and then click the **Open** button.

STEP 10. Click the **Start** button.

STEP 11. Click in the installation window and then at the CentOS 7 screen, either press the **Enter** key to start the installation or wait for the timer to run down and the installation to begin automatically.

> **NOTE** You can press the **Esc** key to avoid the lengthy media check. In addition, to "get out of" the virtual machine, press your right **Ctrl** key (the Ctrl key on the right side of your keyboard).

STEP 12. At the Welcome to CENTOS 7 screen, click the **Continue** button to accept the default installation language, English.

STEP 13. Click the **Installation Destination** button.

STEP 14. Under Local Standard Disks, click on the icon of the **10 GiB** disk multiple times until it is marked as selected. It is marked as selected when a checkmark appears next to the disk icon.

STEP 15. Click the **Done** button in the upper-left area of the window.

STEP 16. Click the **Network & Host Name** button.

STEP 17. Click the icon next to **Ethernet (enp0s3)** to change the value from **OFF** to **ON**.

STEP 18. Click the **Done** button to return to the INSTALLATION SUMMARY screen.

STEP 19. Click the **SOFTWARE SELECTION** button.

STEP 20. Click **GNOME Desktop** and then click the **Done** button.

STEP 21. Click the **Begin Installation** button.

STEP 22. While the installation is running, click on the **ROOT PASSWORD** button and set a password for the root account that is easy for you to remember. You may need to click the **Done** button twice if your password isn't very strong.

STEP 23. While the installation is running, click on the **USER CREATION** button.

STEP 24. For both full name and user name, enter **student**. Enter a password of your choosing and then click the **Done** button. You may need to click the **Done** button twice if your password isn't very strong. Do not make this account an administrator.

STEP 25. When the installation is complete, click the **Reboot** button.

STEP 26. After the system boots, when the INITIAL SETUP screen appears, click the **LICENSE INFORMATION** button.

STEP 27. Click the box next to **I accept the license agreement** and then click the **Done** button in the upper-left corner of the screen.

STEP 28. Click the **FINISH CONFIGURATION** button.

STEP 29. At the login screen, log in as the student user.

STEP 30. After logging in, click the **Next** button at the Welcome screen.

STEP 31. Click the **Next** button at the Typing screen.

STEP 32. Turn off **Location Services** and then click the **Next** button.

STEP 33. Click the **Skip** button at the Online Accounts screen.

STEP 34. Click the **Start using CentOS Linux** button.

STEP 35. If you are interested, you can view the help videos for using GNOME on the Getting Started screen. Close this window when finished.

STEP 36. For the next lab, you need to suspend the CentOS operating system. By suspending, you can start again quickly from the Oracle VirtualBox manager. To suspend, click the close box (the **X**) in the upper-right corner. Make sure **Save the machine state** is selected and then click the **OK** button. When you want to use CentOS again, just double-click the **CENTOS 7 - for class (Saved)** icon in the Oracle VM VirtualBox Manager window.

Lab 1.2 Installing Ubuntu

STEP 1. Go to **https://www.ubuntu.com/download/desktop** and click on the **Download** button.

STEP 2. Click the **Not now, take me to the download** link to download the file. It takes some time to download the file.

STEP 3. Start Oracle VirtualBox and click the **New** button.

STEP 4. Enter **Ubuntu - for class** in the Name box.

STEP 5. Change the memory size to **4196 MB** and click the **Create** button.

STEP 6. Change the file size to **10.00 GB**.

STEP 7. Change the storage on physical hard disk to **Fixed Size** and click the **Create** button.

STEP 8. When you are returned to the main Oracle VirtualBox screen, click the **Start** button.

STEP 9. Click the small folder icon next to the drop-down list and navigate to the location where you downloaded the Ubuntu ISO file. Select that file and then click the **Open** button.

STEP 10. Click the **Start** button.

> **NOTE** The Ubuntu operating system typically doesn't "capture" the mouse, so you shouldn't need to use the right **Ctrl** button to return to the host operating system.

STEP 11. Click the **Install Ubuntu** button.

STEP 12. On the Keyboard layout screen, click the **Continue** button.

STEP 13. On the Updates and other software screen, click the **Continue** button.

STEP 14. On the Installation type screen, click the **Install Now** button.

STEP 15. On the Write the changes to disks? window, click the **Continue** button.

STEP 16. On the Where are you? screen, choose your location and then click the **Continue** button.

STEP 17. On the Who are you? screen, enter **student** in the Your name and Pick a username fields and use whatever you wish for a password. Click the **Continue** button.

STEP 18. When the installation is complete, click the **Restart Now** button.

STEP 19. When prompted to do so, press the **Enter** key.

STEP 20. After the machine has finished booting, log in as the student user.

STEP 21. On the What's new in Ubuntu screen, review the screen and then click the **Next** button.

STEP 22. On the Livepatch screen, click the **Next** button.

STEP 23. On the Help improve Ubuntu screen, click the circle next to No, don't send system info and then click the **Next** button.

STEP 24. On the You're ready to go! screen, click the **Done** button.

STEP 25. If a Software updater screen appears, choose **Install Now**.

STEP 26. For the next lab, you need to suspend the Ubuntu operating system. By suspending, you can start again quickly from the Oracle VirtualBox manager. To suspend, click the close box (the **X**) in the upper-right corner. Make sure **Save the machine state** is selected and then click the **OK** button. When you want to use **Ubuntu** again, just double-click the **Ubuntu - for class (Saved)** icon in the Oracle VM VirtualBox Manager window.

Lab 1.3 Installing Kali

STEP 1. Visit **https://www.kali.org/downloads/** and click the **HTTP** link in the **Kali Linux 64 Bit** row. It takes some time to download the file.

STEP 2. Start Oracle VirtualBox and click the **New** button.

STEP 3. Enter **Kali - for class** in the Name box.

STEP 4. Change the memory size to **4196 MB** and click the **Create** button.

STEP 5. Change the file size to **16.00 GB**.

> **NOTE** The settings in this case are not the same as for the CentOS and Ubuntu installations. Kali Linux has more software and requires a bigger disk.

STEP 6. Change the storage on physical hard disk to **Fixed Size** and click the **Create** button.

STEP 7. When you are returned to the main Oracle VirtualBox screen, click the **Start** button.

STEP 8. Click the small folder icon next to the drop-down list and navigate to the location where you downloaded the Kali ISO file. Select that file and then click the **Open** button.

STEP 9. Click the **Start** button.

> **NOTE** The Kali operating system typically "captures" the mouse, so you will likely need to use the right **Ctrl** button to return to the host operating system.

STEP 10. Use the down arrow key to move to **Graphical install** and press the **Enter** key.

STEP 11. At the Select a language screen, click the **Continue** button.

STEP 12. At the Select your location screen, choose your geographic location.

STEP 13. At the Configure the keyboard screen, click the **Continue** button.

STEP 14. At the first Configure the network screen, click the **Continue** button to accept the default host name.

STEP 15. At the second Configure the network screen, click the **Continue** button leave the domain name blank.

STEP 16. At the Set up users and passwords screen, provide a password of your choosing for the root account.

STEP 17. At the Configure the clock screen, choose your time zone and then click the **Continue** button.

STEP 18. At the first Partition disks screen, click the **Continue** button to use the default **Guided - use entire disk** option.

STEP 19. At the second Partition disks screen, click the **Continue** button to use the available disk.

STEP 20. At the third Partition disks screen, click the **Continue** button to use the default **All files in one partition** option.

STEP 21. At the fourth Partition disks screen, click the **Continue** button to use the default **Finish partitioning and write changes to disk** option.

STEP 22. At the fifth Partition disks screen, click the circle next to **Yes** and then click the **Continue** button.

STEP 23. On the first Configure the package manager screen, click the **Continue** button.

STEP 24. On the second Configure the package manager screen, click the **Continue** button.

STEP 25. On the first Install the GRUB boot loader on a hard disk screen, click the **Continue** button.

STEP 26. On the second Install the GRUB boot loader on a hard disk screen, click on the line that starts with **/dev/sda** and then click the **Continue** button.

STEP 27. On the Finish the installation screen, click the **Continue** button.

STEP 28. After the system has rebooted, log in as the root user.

STEP 29. For the next lab, you need to suspend the Kali operating system. By suspending, you can start again quickly from the Oracle VirtualBox manager. To suspend, click the close box (the **X**) in the upper-right corner. Make sure **Save the machine state** is selected and then click the **OK** button. When you want to use Kali again, just double-click the **Kali - for class (Saved)** icon in the Oracle VM VirtualBox Manager window.

Chapter 2

Working on the Command Line

These labs should be performed on the Ubuntu operating system that you installed in Chapter 1, "Distributions and Key Components." Before you begin this lab, log in to the student account that you created during the installation process.

Lab 2.1 Manage Files

STEP 1. Open a terminal window.

_____

STEP 2. Display your current directory.

_____

STEP 3. Using an absolute pathname, switch to the **/etc** directory.

_____

STEP 4. Using a relative pathname, move to the **/etc/skel** directory.

_____

STEP 5. Using a relative pathname, move up one directory.

_____

STEP 6. List the files in the current directory.

_____

STEP 7. Perform a "long display" listing of the files in the current directory.

_____

STEP 8. List all the files in the current directory that begin with the letter _s_.

_____

STEP 9. Run the command that will determine the type of contents in the **/etc/group** file.

_____

STEP 10. Display only the last five lines of the **/etc/group** file.

_____

STEP 11. Execute the command to return to your home directory.

_____

STEP 12. Make a directory named **data** in the current directory.

_____

STEP 13. Copy the **/etc/passwd** file into the data directory.

_____

STEP 14. Copy the **/etc/ppp** directory into the current directory (and ignore any "Permission denied" error messages).

_____

STEP 15. Rename the **ppp** directory that is located in the current directory to **peers**.

_____

STEP 16. Update the timestamp of the **data/passwd** file to the current date and time.

_____

STEP 17. Create a new empty file named **test** in the **data** directory.

_____

STEP 18. Delete the data/passwd file.

_____

STEP 19. Delete the **peers** directory.

_____

Lab 2.2 Using Shell Features

STEP 1. Open a terminal window.

_____

STEP 2. Display the value of the **HOME** variable.

_____

STEP 3. Display all the shell variables and values.

_____

STEP 4. Display the value of the **TEST** variable. (Note that this variable currently has no value.)

_____

STEP 5. Change the current shell so that an error message will be displayed when an undefined variable is used.

_____

STEP 6. Modify the **PATH** variable to include the **/opt** directory.

_____

STEP 7. Create a new environment variable named **EVENT** and set it to the value **"now"** by using a single command.

_____

STEP 8. Display all the environment variables.

_____

STEP 9. Create an alias in the current shell for the **ls** command so it will run the command **ls -a**.

_____

STEP 10. Display all the aliases for the current shell.

_____

STEP 11. Remove the **fgrep** alias from the current shell.

_____

STEP 12. Display a list of previously executed commands.

STEP 13. Re-execute the last **ls** command from the history list.

STEP 14. Change the maximum number of commands stored in the history list for the current shell to a value of **2000**.

STEP 15. Execute the **ps -fe** command and pipe the output to the **less** command.

STEP 16. List all filenames in the **/etc** directory structure (including subdirectories) that are group owned by the **lp** group.

STEP 17. Display all the files in the **/etc/passwd** file that contain at least three sequential numbers.

STEP 18. Display the **/etc/passwd** file with all occurrences of **root** replaced with **XXXX**.

Lab 2.3 Compressing Files

STEP 1. Open a terminal window.

STEP 2. While using the verbose feature, create a tar file named **ppp.tar** that contains the contents of the **/etc/ppp** directory. (Ignore any error messages.)

STEP 3. List the contents of the **ppp.tar** file.

STEP 4. Create a directory named **tar_data** in the current directory.

STEP 5. Extract the contents of the **ppp.tar** file into the **tar_data** directory.

STEP 6. Compress the **ppp.tar** file by using the **gzip** command but don't overwrite the existing **ppp.tar** file; rather, create a new file named **ppp.tar.gz**.

STEP 7. Compress the **ppp.tar** file with the **bzip2** command but don't overwrite the existing **ppp.tar** file; rather, create a new file named **ppp.tar.bz2**.

_____

STEP 8. Compare the size of the **ppp.tar.gz** and **ppp.tar.bz2** files to determine which one is smaller.

_____

STEP 9. Delete the **ppp.tar** file.

_____

STEP 10. Unzip the **ppp.tar.gz** file.

_____

Chapter 3

Getting Help

These labs should be performed on the Ubuntu operating system that you installed in Chapter 1, "Distributions and Key Components." Before you begin this lab, log in to the student account that you created during the installation process.

Lab 3.1 Getting Help with *man*

STEP 1. Open a terminal window.

STEP 2. Display the man page for the **ls** command.

STEP 3. Search for the term *sort*.

STEP 4. Continue the search until you find the option to sort by file size.

STEP 5. Quit the man page.

STEP 6. Determine which sections the **ls** command is in.

STEP 7. Search the man pages for the keyword list and pipe the output to the **less** command.

STEP 8. Execute the **su -** command to switch to the root account. (Enter the root password when prompted.)

STEP 9. Run the command to update the man page databases.

STEP 10. Run the **exit** command to return to the student account.

STEP 11. Change the **MANPATH** variable to include the **/var/man** directory.

STEP 12. Execute the **ls** command with the option to display help information for the command.

STEP 13. Use the **help** command to display information about the **umask** command.

Lab 3.2 Getting Help with *info*

STEP 1. Open a terminal window.

_____

STEP 2. Execute the **info** command with no arguments.

_____

STEP 3. Go to the File permissions section.

_____

STEP 4. Go to the Mode Structure section.

_____

STEP 5. Enter the command to move to the next node (which should be node 27.2).

_____

STEP 6. Enter the command to return to the previous node (which should be node 27.1).

_____

STEP 7. Enter the command to return to the parent node (which should be node 27).

_____

STEP 8. Enter the command to return to the node you were last in (which should be 27.1).

_____

STEP 9. Quit the info pages.

_____

> **NOTE** From this point on, you may need to view man or info pages in order to complete the labs.

Chapter 4

Editing Files

These labs should be performed on the Ubuntu operating system that you installed in Chapter 1, "Distributions and Key Components." Before you begin this lab, log in to the student account that you created during the installation process.

Answers may vary in this lab, as there are multiple ways to accomplish various tasks in **vim**.

Lab 4.1 Editing Files with the *vim* Editor

STEP 1. Open a terminal window.

_____

STEP 2. Copy the **/usr/share/doc/git-doc/user-manual.txt** file into your current directory (This file was chosen because it is on the system by default and is a rather large file.)

_____

STEP 3. Open the **user-manual.txt** file in a **vim** editor.

_____

STEP 4. Move down 12 lines

_____

STEP 5. In insert mode, enter the following: *****

_____

STEP 6. Return to the command mode.

_____

STEP 7. Go to line 43.

_____

_____

STEP 8. Delete the current line.

_____

STEP 9. Move down one line.

_____

STEP 10. Open a new line below the current line.

_____

STEP 11. Enter the following text into the document: Review this data

_____

STEP 12. Return to the command mode.

_____

STEP 13. Go to the top of the file.

_____

_____

STEP 14. Move forward three sentences.

_____

STEP 15. Move forward four words.

_____

STEP 16. Search for the term *example*.

_____

STEP 17. Continue to the next occurrence of the search term.

_____

STEP 18. Delete the current word.

_____

STEP 19. Go to the end of the document.

_____

STEP 20. Paste the text from the buffer at the end of the current line.

_____

STEP 21. Return to the top of the document.

_____

STEP 22. Replace all occurrences of *project* with *program* throughout the document.

_____

STEP 23. Save and quit the document.

_____

STEP 24. Run the **vimtutor** program and then read and follow all the steps in that program.

_____

Chapter 5

When Things Go Wrong

These labs should be performed on the Ubuntu operating system that you installed in Chapter 1, "Distributions and Key Components." Before you begin this lab, log in to the student account that you created during the installation process.

Lab 5.1 Troubleshooting Linux Issues

You won't find the answers for this lab directly in the book. Troubleshooting requires exploring and reading documentation—skills you will develop during this lab.

STEP 1. Open a terminal window.

_____

STEP 2. Execute the command **ls /var/logs**.

_____

STEP 3. The command from step 2 fails. Review the error message and determine why.

_____

STEP 4. What command could you run to determine the correct directory name?

_____

_____

STEP 5. Execute the correct command to view the directory that contains the logs.

_____

STEP 6. Run the command **head -N 7 /etc/passwd**.

_____

STEP 7. The command from step 6 fails. What command could you use to determine the right option?

_____

STEP 8. Execute the correct command, based on what you learned by reading the documentation.

_____

STEP 9. Execute the following command: **cp /etc/passwd /var**.

_____

STEP 10. The command from step 9 fails. What command could you use to determine the right option?

_____

STEP 11. Based on why the command failed, determine a location where you can copy this file and run the correct command.

_____

Lab 5.2 Configuring User Notifications

STEP 1. Open a terminal window.

STEP 2. Use the **su -** command to switch to the root user account (using the password you set during the installation process for the root user).

STEP 3. Modify the correct file to change the command-line login prompt to display the current date, the node name, and the number of users currently logged in to the system.

STEP 4. Modify the correct file to change the network login prompt to display the message *Welcome to this system.*

STEP 5. Modify the correct file to display the network login prompt from step 4 when an SSH connection is made.

STEP 6. Execute the following command to restart the SSH server and enable the changes made in step 5: **service ssh restart**.

STEP 7. Open a new terminal window.

STEP 8. Test the SSH prompt by logging in to the remote system: **ssh localhost**.

STEP 9. Enter the **exit** command to log out of the SSH connection. (Run this command only once; running it a second time will result in your terminal window being closed.)

STEP 10. Return to your original window, in which you are logged in as the root user. (Keep the terminal window from step 7 open.) Create a message-of-the-day file that displays *Restricted server - only log in if you have been authorized* after a user logs in.

STEP 11. Return to the terminal window that you opened in step 7 and run the **ssh localhost** command again to test the message-of-the-day file.

STEP 12. Enter the **exit** command to log out of the SSH connection. (Run this command only once; running it a second time will result in your terminal window being closed.)

STEP 13. Return to your original window in which you are logged in as the root user. (Keep the terminal window from step 7 open.) Try to send a message to all terminal windows that says *Meeting starts in 5 minutes* by executing the following command: **wall Meeting starts in 5 minutes**

_____

STEP 14. The command in step 13 fails. Review the output of the command and documentation. When you have identified the problem, perform the steps needed to send the **wall** message to all terminal windows.

_____

_____

_____

STEP 15. Re-send the broadcast message from step 14 without displaying the banner information.

_____

STEP 16. Return to the other terminal window that you opened in step 7 and stop wall messages from being displayed.

_____

STEP 17. In the terminal window that you are logged in to as the root user, issue a **shutdown** command but use the option that will not actually cause the system to shut down.

_____

Chapter 6

Managing Group Accounts

These labs should be performed on the Ubuntu operating system that you installed in Chapter 1, "Distributions and Key Components." Before you begin this lab, log in to the student account that you created during the installation process.

Lab 6.1 Managing Group Accounts

STEP 1. Open a terminal window.

STEP 2. Display the current user's ID and group membership.

STEP 3. Display the group membership of the root account.

STEP 4. Run the correct command to determine the user owner and group owner of the **/etc/group** file.

STEP 5. Display the group account information for the games group.

STEP 6. Display the group password information for the games group.

STEP 7. Run the **su -** following command to switch to the root account (and provide the root password when prompted).

STEP 8. Create a new group named test.

STEP 9. Display the group account information for the test group.

STEP 10. Change the group name of the test group to newtest.

STEP 11. Add the student account as a secondary member of the newtest group without overriding this user's current group membership.

Lab 6.2 Managing Group Administrators

Scenario: In this lab you will be asked to provide a "goal" rather than be told specifically which steps to take. It is up to you to achieve the end result based on what you have learned regarding this topic. Create a new group named eng and add the student user to this group. Make the student user a group administrator. To test this, add the bin user to the eng group while logged in as the student user and then verify this new group membership.

_____

_____

_____

_____

_____

_____

_____

_____

_____

_____

_____

_____

_____

_____

_____

_____

_____

_____

_____

Chapter 7

Managing User Accounts

These labs should be performed on the Ubuntu operating system that you installed in Chapter 1, "Distributions and Key Components." Before you begin this lab, log in to the student account that you created during the installation process.

Lab 7.1 Managing User Accounts

STEP 1. Open a terminal window.

STEP 2. Execute the correct command to display user account information (including the login shell and home directory) for the bin account.

STEP 3. Execute the correct command to display user password information (including the encrypted password and password aging) for the bin account.

STEP 4. The command in step 3 should have failed. Execute the correct **su** command to change your account so the command from step 3 will be successful when executed.

STEP 5. Create a new user named jake and explicitly use options to create the home directory **/home/jake** for this user.

STEP 6. Set a password for the jake user to a password of your choosing.

STEP 7. Run the correct command to display the default values used when a new account is created.

STEP 8. Using the **less** command, display the file that contains the password aging defaults.

STEP 9. Using the **less** command, display the file that contains the default login shell.

STEP 10. Delete the jake user and his home directory, using a single command.

Lab 7.2 Securing User Accounts

WARNING   With Ubuntu, some of the options for user account commands are different from the standard options provided in the book. For this lab you need to explore the documentation for the specific Ubuntu distro you installed to discover the correct answer.

Scenario: Create a user account named sue with the following restrictions:

- The account should have a strong, randomly generated password (consider using https://passwordsgenerator.net or a similar site to create the password).
- The user should be a secondary member of the games group.
- The user's home directory should be explicitly set as **/home/sue**.
- The user should be forced to change her password every 60 days.
- The user should not be allowed to change her password for 2 days after it has been set.
- The password warning field should be set to 10.
- The password inactivity period should be set to 60.
- The account should be set to expire on January 1, 2025.
- This user (and all others) should have a minimum password length of 12 characters.

_____

_____

_____

_____

_____

_____

_____

_____

_____

_____

_____

_____

_____

_____

_____

_____

_____

_____

_____

_____

_____

Lab 7.3 Configuring *sudo*

Scenario: Allow the sue user the ability to use the **apt-get** command. Verify this ability by installing the joe package as the sue user.

Chapter 8

Develop an Account Security Policy

These labs should be performed on the Kali operating system that you installed in Chapter 1, "Distributions and Key Components." Before you begin this lab, log in to the student account that you created during the installation process.

Lab 8.1 Testing the Security of Accounts

Scenario: Create five user accounts, with a different password for each account. Make some of the passwords very simple, such as simple words, and some of the passwords more complex. Then run the johnny password attack tool on these new accounts and see which passwords were compromised by the tool.

_____

_____

_____

_____

_____

_____

_____

_____

_____

_____

_____

_____

_____

_____

_____

_____

_____

_____

_____

_____

_____

_____

_____

_____

_____

_____

_____

Lab 8.2 Developing an Account Security Policy

This lab does not have a specific correct answer. The goal is to use what you learned in Chapters 6, 7, and 8 of *Linux Essentials for Cybersecurity* to develop security policies for user and group accounts.

As a starting point, you can make use of some excellent sample security policies located at https://www.sans.org/security-resources/policies. You may find some policies on this site very useful, as some are specific to accounts. For example, there is a policy called Password Protection Policy. While you can make use of some of the policies on this site and make use of the format of the policies, you should also include original work that you create, based on what you have learned in Chapters 6, 7, and 8 of *Linux Essentials for Cybersecurity*.

_____

_____

_____

_____

_____

_____

_____

_____

_____

_____

_____

_____

_____

_____

_____

_____

_____

_____

_____

_____

_____

_____

Chapter 9

File Permissions

These labs should be performed on the CentOS operating system that you installed in Chapter 1, "Distributions and Key Components." Before you begin this lab, log in to the student account that you created during the installation process.

Lab 9.1 Managing File Permissions

STEP 1. Open a terminal window.

_____

STEP 2. Execute the correct command to display the permissions on the **/etc/chrony.keys** file.

_____

STEP 3. Based on the output of the command from step 2, which user owns the **/etc/chrony.keys** file?

_____

STEP 4. Based on the output of the command from step 2, which group owns the **/etc/chrony.keys** file?

_____

STEP 5. Execute the **more/etc/chrony.keys** command and then explain why the command failed.

_____

STEP 6. Switch to the root account using the **su** command.

_____

STEP 7. Execute the correct command to add the student user to the chrony group.

_____

STEP 8. Log out of the system. (Note that this is necessary for the group ownership to take effect.)

_____

STEP 9. Log in as the student user.

_____

STEP 10. Open a terminal window.

_____

STEP 11. Execute the correct command to display the current user's groups.

_____

_____

STEP 12. Execute the **more/etc/chrony.keys** command to verify that this file's contents can now be displayed by the student user.

_____

STEP 13. Copy the **/etc/chrony.keys** file to the current directory (the home directory for the student user).

_____

STEP 14. Using octal notation, change the permissions of the **chrony.keys** file that is in the current directory to **-r---------**.

_____

STEP 15. Using symbolic notation, change the permissions of the **chrony.keys** file that is in the current directory to allow group members the read permission.

_____

STEP 16. Using octal notation, try to change the permissions of the **chrony.keys** file that is in the **/etc** directory to **-r--------**. Explain why this command fails.

_____

STEP 17. Change the mask value for the current shell so any new directory would have the following permissions: **drwxr-x---**

_____

STEP 18. Based on the mask value from step 17, what permissions would all new files that are created in this shell have?

_____

Lab 9.2 Managing Special Permissions

Scenario 1: You are concerned about SUID permissions on this system. Start by running the command to find all files that have SUID permissions set. Then change the **newgrp** command so it is not a SUID file.

_____

_____

_____

Scenario 2: Three users need to share files on the system, but no other user can have access to these files. Create user accounts for sophia, olivia, and emma, using default values for account parameters. Create a common group named shared, which will be used to allow these three users to share files with each other. Finally, create a directory named **/home/shared** for only these three users to access and to also automatically give group ownership of all new files to the shared group.

_____

_____

_____

_____

Scenario 3: Create a directory named **/data** in which all users can add files to share with others. This directory should only allow a file to be deleted by the owner of the file (and the root user).

_____

_____

_____

Lab 9.3 Enabling Access Control Lists

STEP 1. Open a terminal window.

_____

STEP 2. Copy the **/etc/hosts** file to the student user's home directory.

_____

STEP 3. Set an access control list (ACL) for the games group that allows read and write permissions for that group on the **hosts** file.

_____

_____

STEP 4. Display the ACLs for the **hosts** file.

_____

STEP 5. Change the ACL mask value to read-only for the **hosts** file.

_____

_____

STEP 6. Display the ACLs for the **hosts** file to verify the ACL mask.

_____

STEP 7. Create a directory called **test_acl**.

_____

STEP 8. Create a default ACL for the **test_acl** directory so the adm user has read and write permissions for all new files and directories created in the **test_acl** directory.

_____

_____

STEP 9. Use the **touch** command to create a new file named **test_file** in the **test_acl** directory.

_____

STEP 10. Verify the default ACLs by viewing the ACLs for the **test_file** file.

_____

Lab 9.4 Managing File Ownership and Attributes

STEP 1. Open a terminal window.

_____

STEP 2. Use the **su** command to switch to the root account.

_____

STEP 3. Copy the **/etc/group** file to the **/tmp** directory.

_____

STEP 4. Change the user ownership of the **/tmp/group** file to the student user.

_____

STEP 5. Change the group ownership of the **/tmp/group** file to the bin group.

_____

STEP 6. Make the **/tmp/group** file immutable.

_____

STEP 7. Run the correct command to display the file attributes of the **/tmp/group** file.

_____

STEP 8. Attempt to remove the **/tmp/group** file. Explain why this fails.

_____

STEP 9. Remove the immutable attribute from the **/tmp/group** file.

_____

STEP 10. Remove the /tmp/group file.

_____

Lab 9.5 Monitoring Security Issues with SELinux

STEP 1. Open a terminal window.

_____

STEP 2. Use the **su** command to switch to the root account.

_____

STEP 3. Execute the correct command to determine what mode (enforcing or permissive) SELinux is currently in.

_____

> **NOTE**   CentOS normally defaults to enforcing mode.

STEP 4. Change the current mode to permissive.

_____

STEP 5. Display any log entries related to SELinux.

_____

STEP 6.   Change the current mode to enforcing.

_____

> **NOTE**   SELinux prevents access to files, so it is somewhat similar to permissions and file attributes. However, it is normally used in conjunction with servers, such as FTP and web servers. As a result, more SELinux content will appear later in this book.

Chapter | 10

Manage Local Storage: Essentials

These labs should be performed on the CentOS operating system that you installed in Chapter 1, "Distributions and Key Components." Before you begin this lab, log in to the student account that you created during the installation process.

Lab 10.1 Creating Partitions and Filesystems

STEP 1. Open a terminal window.

_____

STEP 2. Use the **su** command to switch to the root user.

_____

STEP 3. Execute the **ls /dev/sd*** command to see the current hard disk devices. There should be a **/dev/sda** hard disk and two partitions: **/dev/sda1** and **/dev/sda2**.

_____

STEP 4. Execute the **shutdown now** command to power off the operating system.

_____

STEP 5. In the Oracle VM VirtualBox Manager program, right-click the **CENTOS 7 - for class** VM and then click **Settings**, as shown in the following graphic:

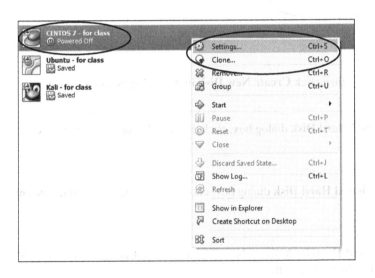

_____

STEP 6. Click **Storage** and then click the **Controller: SATA** section to highlight that section. Then click the small **add** icon, as shown in the following graphic:

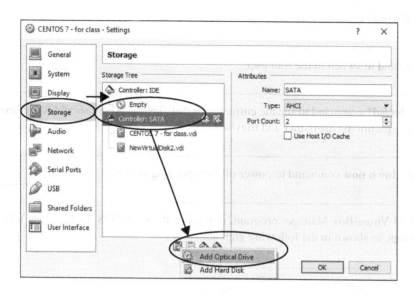

STEP 7. Click **Add Hard Disk** and then click **Create New Disk** in the dialog box that appears.

STEP 8. In the first **Create Virtual Hard Disk** dialog box, click the **Next** button to accept the default option, **VDI**.

STEP 9. In the second **Create Virtual Hard Disk** dialog box, click the circle next to **Fixed Size** and then click the **Next** button.

STEP 10. In the third **Create Virtual Hard Disk** dialog box, change the size from the default of 8GB to 100MB and then click the **Create** button.

STEP 11. Click the **OK** button to close the **Settings** dialog box. You should now have another hard disk for practicing partitioning.

STEP 12. Double-click the **CENTOS 7 - for class** VM to start the virtual machine.

STEP 13. After the boot process completes, log in as the student user.

STEP 14. Open a terminal window.

STEP 15. Use the **su** command to switch to the root user.

_____

STEP 16. Execute the **ls /dev/sd*** command to see the new hard disk device. The new device is the **/dev/sdb** file.

_____

STEP 17. Execute the correct **fdisk** command to display the partition table of **/dev/sda** (which should display two partitions).

_____

STEP 18. Execute the correct **fdisk** command to display the partition table of **/dev/sdb** (one of which should be empty).

_____

_____

STEP 19. Use the **fdisk** command to create a new primary partition on the **/dev/sdb** device. The size of this new partition should be 25MB.

_____

_____

_____

_____

_____

_____

_____

_____

_____

_____

_____

_____

_____

_____

STEP 20. Create an ext4 filesystem on the **/dev/sdb1** partition.

_____

STEP 21. Make a directory named **/repo** and mount the **/dev/sdb1** partition under this directory.

_____

_____

> **NOTE** Do not destroy this partition. You will use it in the next lab.

Lab 10.2 Mounting Filesystems at Boot

Scenario: You now have a new partition (**/dev/sdb1**) with an ext4 filesystem mounted under **/repo**. Configure the system so this partition will automatically be mounted during the boot process. Use the following parameters:

- Assign the label **repo** to the filesystem. Use the label, not the device name, to perform the mount.
- For mount options, do not allow SUID programs on this filesystem.
- For FSCK check, use the value **1**.
- For dump level, use the value **0**.

Configure the system for this automatic mount and then test the mount before rebooting the system.

_____

_____

_____

_____

_____

_____

_____

_____

_____

_____

_____

_____

_____

_____

_____

_____

_____

_____

_____

_____

NOTE   Do not destroy this partition. You will use it in the next lab.

Lab 10.3 Managing Swap Devices

Scenario: Create two new swap devices. One swap device should be a 50MB file named **/var/swapfile**. The second swap device should be a swap partition (**/dev/sdb2**) that is 50MB in size. These swap devices should be automatically enabled during each boot process. (Use the UUID of the partition for this.)

Chapter 11

Manage Local Storage: Advanced Features

These labs should be performed on the CentOS operating system that you installed in Chapter 1, "Distributions and Key Components." Before you begin this lab, log in to the student account that you created during the installation process.

Lab 11.1 Managing Encrypted Filesystems

Scenario: In Lab 10.1 you created a partition that was mounted under the **/repo** directory. Change this partition so it has an encrypted filesystem on it. Note that the aes and sha256 modules do not need to be loaded for CentOS.

After you complete this lab, you can remove the line that you added to the **/etc/fstab** file as you will not be using this partition in any further lab.

Lab 11.2 Configuring Logical Volumes

Scenario: Add three new 50MB virtual hard disks to your system to simulate a server that has three new hard drives. Use the technique provided in Lab 10.1 to create these new hard disks within the Oracle VM VirtualBox Manager program. Then create a new volume group named VG1, using these three hard drives. Using the VG1 volume group, create two logical volumes: a logical volume named **lv0** that is 20MB in size, and a logical volume named **lv1** that uses the rest of the available space from VG1. Create filesystems for each new logical volume, create mount points (**/lv0** and **/lv1**), and configure the system to mount these new logical volumes during the boot process.

Lab 11.3 Administering Disk Quotas

Scenario: Implement disk quotas on the filesystem that is mounted under the **/lv1** mount point. The limitations should be for the student user. Apply a hard limit on this user account of 10MB of file space and 100 files. Also create a soft limit of 8MB and 80 files.

Lab 11.4 Managing Hard and Soft Links

STEP 1. Open a terminal window.

_____

STEP 2. Switch to the root account by using the **su** command.

_____

STEP 3. Using the **ls** and **grep** commands, display all the soft links in the **/var** directory.

_____

STEP 4. Create a soft line from a file named **/root/info** to the **/etc/passwd** file.

_____

STEP 5. Execute the correct command to display the soft link you created in step 4.

_____

STEP 6. Execute the correct command to display the number of hard links for the **/usr/bin/c2ph** file.

_____

STEP 7. Execute the correct command to display the inode number of the **/usr/bin/c2ph** file.

_____

STEP 8. Execute the correct command to find all the files that are hard linked with the **/usr/bin/c2ph** file.

_____

_____

Chapter 12

Manage Network Storage

These labs should be performed on the CentOS operating system that you installed in Chapter 1, "Distributions and Key Components." Before you begin this lab, log in to the student account that you created during the installation process.

> **NOTE** Ideally you would have two systems for working on network-based labs. However, such a setup would require extra RAM and a faster CPU. To avoid having too many hardware requirements for your system, this lab has you run a single virtual machine that acts as both the server and the client.

Lab 12.1 Configuring Samba

STEP 1. Open a terminal window.

STEP 2. Use the **su** command to switch to the root user.

STEP 3. Install the **samba** package by using the **yum** command.

STEP 4. Edit the configuration file for the Samba server by using the **vim** command.

STEP 5. Add a share for the **/usr/bin** directory called **commands**. This should be a read-only share that is browseable.

STEP 6. Execute the correct command to check the syntax and format of the Samba server configuration file.

STEP 7. Execute the following commands to start the Samba services and ensure that they will start at boot:

```
systemctl enable smb
systemctl enable nmb
systemctl start smb
systemctl start nmb
```

STEP 8. Create a Samba account for the student user. Provide a password of your choosing.

STEP 9. Use the student Samba account to display the Samba server shares of the local machine (using localhost or 127.0.0.1 for the server name or IP address).

STEP 10. Connect to the Samba **commands** share by using the **smbclient** command.

_____

STEP 11. At the **smb** prompt, list the files on the share.

_____

STEP 12. Quit the **smbclient** utility.

_____

STEP 13. Make a directory named **/commands**.

_____

STEP 14. Mount the Samba **commands** share by using the student account under the **/commands** directory.

_____

STEP 15. List the files in the **/commands** directory to verify that the mount worked currently.

_____

STEP 16. Unmount the Samba share.

_____

> **NOTE**   Consider how you would mount this resource automatically during the reboot process but do not make this change to your system. The Samba service starts after the mounting process, and mounting the resource automatically during the reboot process could cause issues with booting. Mounting a remote Samba share during the reboot process would be a more realistic scenario.

Lab 12.2 Administering NFS

> **NOTE** CentOS 7 uses NFS version 4, which does not use the **portmap** utility. As a result, you should not start the **portmap** service in this lab.

Scenario: Create an NFS share of the **/usr/bin** directory. The share should be available for all machines as a read-only share. Test this share locally by mounting the resource manually using the **/commands** directory created in Lab 12.1. When you are finished, unmount the resource.

_____

_____

_____

_____

_____

_____

_____

_____

_____

_____

_____

_____

_____

_____

Lab 12.3 Managing iSCSI

STEP 1. Open a terminal window.

_____

STEP 2. Use the **su** command to switch to the root user.

_____

STEP 3. Use the following **yum** commands to install the packages that allow you to create iSCSI targets on CentOS 7:

```
yum install epel-release
yum install scsi-target-utils
```

_____

_____

STEP 4. To use the **/dev/sdb1** partition that you created in Lab 10.1 for the iSCSI target, start by umounting the partition.

_____

STEP 5. Next, remove the line in the **/etc/fstab** file that mounts this device automatically at boot.

_____

STEP 6. Add the correct entry in the file **/etc/tgt/targets.conf** to share the **/dev/sdb1** device using the IP address 127.0.0.1 for the permitted initiator.

_____

_____

_____

_____

_____

_____

_____

_____

STEP 7. Start and enable the **tgtd** daemon by executing the following commands:

```
systemctl enable tgtd
systemctl start tgtd
```

STEP 8. Execute the correct command to verify that the target has been enabled on this system.

_____

STEP 9. Execute the correct command to display the targets provided by the iSCSI server with IP address 127.0.0.1.

_____

> **NOTE**   Because having an iSCSI target and initiator on the same system may cause issues, this lab stops at this point. Review the content in Chapter 12 of _Linux Essentials for Cybersecurity_ for a look at the steps required to make use of this iSCSI device.

Chapter 13

Develop a Storage Security Policy

These labs should be performed on the CentOS operating system that you installed in Chapter 1, "Distributions and Key Components." Before you begin this lab, log in to the student account that you created during the installation process.

Lab 13.1 Backing Up a Filesystem

STEP 1. Open a terminal window.

STEP 2. Use the **su** command to switch to the root user.

STEP 3. Back up the contents of the **/etc/X11** directory into a tar file named **/tmp/X11.tar**.

STEP 4. List the contents of the **/tmp/X11.tar** file, including details about the files (such as using verbose mode).

STEP 5. Move to the **/tmp** directory.

STEP 6. Extract the contents of the **X11.tar** file into the current directory.

STEP 7. Back up the contents of the **/etc/X11** directory into a compressed tar file named **/tmp/X11.tar.gz**, using the gzip compression option.

STEP 8. Execute the correct command so that you can see and compare the sizes of the two tar files.

Lab 13.2 Developing a Backup Security Policy

This lab does not have a specific correct answer. Your goal is to use what you have learned in Chapters 9, 10, 11, and 12 of *Linux Essentials for Cybersecurity* to develop security policies for backing up data.

As a starting point, you can make use of some excellent sample security policies available at https://www.sans.org/security-resources/policies. You may find some policies at this site very useful, as some are specific to accounts. For example, there is a sample policy called Disaster Recovery Plan Policy. While you can make use of some of the policies on this site and make use of the format of the policies, you should also include original work that you create, based on what you have learned in Chapters 9, 10, 11, and 12 of *Linux Essentials for Cybersecurity*.

_____

_____

_____

_____

_____

_____

_____

_____

_____

_____

_____

_____

_____

_____

_____

_____

_____

_____

_____

_____

_____

Chapter 14

Crontab and At

These labs should be performed on the Ubuntu operating system that you installed in Chapter 1, "Distributions and Key Components." Before you begin this lab, log in to the student account that you created during the installation process.

Lab 14.1 Managing *crontab*

STEP 1. Open a terminal window.

STEP 2. Execute the command that will allow you to edit the current user's **crontab** file.

STEP 3. After you have entered the editor, add a **crontab** entry that will run the **who** command at 5:50 p.m. every weekday (Monday through Friday) and send the output of the command to the **/home/student/who-there** file.

STEP 4. Save your changes and exit the editor.

STEP 5. Execute the command that will allow you to view the current user's **crontab** file.

STEP 6. Use the **su** command to switch to the root account.

STEP 7. Execute the command that will allow you to view the student user's **crontab** file.

STEP 8. Modify the system so the student user can no longer use the **crontab** command.

STEP 9. Execute the command to return to the student account.

STEP 10. Execute the command that will allow you to view the current user's **crontab** file. Note that this command should fail because of the action you took in step 8.

STEP 11. Use the **su** command to switch to the root account.

STEP 12. Execute the command that will allow you to view the student user's **crontab** file (and read the message that tells why this command fails). Note that while the student user can no longer execute **crontab** commands, the previous **crontab** entry for this user still exists.

STEP 13. Execute the command to view the **/var/spool/cron/crontabs/student** file. Note that this command has the same output as **crontab -l -u student** when the student user still had access to the **crontab** command. This is because this file is where the student user's **crontab** file is stored.

STEP 14. Delete the **/var/spool/cron/crontabs/student** file and then use the **systemctl restart cron** command to restart the **crontab** service.

_____

_____

STEP 15. View the primary system **crontab** file. You will not be making changes to this file, but based on what you see in this file, describe the tasks that are performed.

_____

_____

_____

_____

_____

STEP 16. Execute the correct command to view the commands that will be executed by the system **crontab** once per day.

_____

STEP 17. Execute the correct command that displays the content of the directory that holds _additional_ system **crontab** entries.

_____

Lab 14.2 Configuring *at* Commands

STEP 1. Open a terminal window.

_____

STEP 2. Using the **at** command, execute a command at 2 p.m. tomorrow. You will be removing this **at** job, so the actual command is not really important. For example, you can execute the **ls** command.

_____

_____

STEP 3. List the **at** jobs for the current user.

_____

STEP 4. Remove the **at** job you created in step 2.

_____

Chapter 15

Scripting

These labs should be performed on the Ubuntu operating system that you installed in Chapter 1, "Distributions and Key Components." Before you begin this lab, log in to the student account that you created during the installation process.

> **NOTE** When reviewing the lab answers for this chapter, keep in mind that when it comes to creating programs, there is not any single correct answer. If your program meets the goal of the scenario, then you have completed the task correctly, even if your answer differs from the answer provided. One could argue that there is a best answer, but what is "best" may vary depending on what is most important (for example, speed of the program, memory utilization). However, for these labs, the goal is to meet the objective stated in the scenario.

Lab 15.1 Script Project #1

Scenario: In some cases, people who are not strong in Linux may need to run specific Linux commands. To make this easier, you can create a menu-driven program that runs these Linux commands. Such a program allows users to execute the commands without having to actually know about how to execute them.

For this scenario, create a menu-driven program that has the following options:

1. List users who are logged in (using the **who** command)
2. List system information (using the **uname -v** command)
3. List the five largest files in the current directory (using the **ls -lS** command)
4. List basic CPU information (using the **lscpu | head** command)
5. Display system time (using the **date** command)
6. Exit the program

The program should continue in a loop until the user chooses option 6. The program should also produce an error message if an invalid option is chosen.

Lab 15.2 Script Project #2

Scenario: Often one of the biggest challenges with a script is validating user input. Even simple things like ensuring that a valid integer is entered can result in a fair amount of code.

For this scenario, create a program that validates user input so that only an integer (whole number), positive or negative, is allowed.

_____

_____

_____

_____

_____

_____

_____

_____

_____

_____

_____

_____

_____

_____

_____

_____

_____

_____

_____

_____

_____

_____

_____

_____

_____

_____

Chapter 16

Common Automation Tasks

These labs should be performed on the Ubuntu operating system that you installed in Chapter 1, "Distributions and Key Components." Before you begin this lab, log in to the student account that you created during the installation process.

Lab 16.1 Script Project #3

Scenario: Performing system checks manually can be time consuming, and the process is oven overlooked. For this scenario, create a shell script that searches the entire system for the following files:

- SUID files
- SGID files (not directories)
- Files and directories that have the write permission set for the "others" permission set, not including symbolic links.

This script should create a report in the **/var/reports** directory. The report should include all the aforementioned files, and the filename should be **file-report-*date***, where *date* is replaced with the current system date (for example, **file-report-10-22-2019**).

Test the script as the root user and then have this script run nightly at 3:15 a.m. by adding a file in the **/etc/cron.d** directory.

_____

_____

_____

_____

_____

_____

_____

_____

_____

_____

_____

_____

_____

_____

_____

_____

_____

_____

_____

_____

Lab 16.2 Script Project #4

Scenario: Users in your organization have complained that it takes too long for IT support to assist them when they need to get a backup file restored. They want to be able to restore files on their own when they accidently delete files. There are several possible solutions to this situation, including a feature called "backup snapshots" that you should look into when you have a chance. However, because there are only a handful of people on this system, a simple script should work.

Create a script that will back up all the files of every user's home directory (except the "root" user) in **tar** format. These backups should go into a directory named **/var/backups/***username*, where *username* is replaced by the name of the user.

> **NOTE** Consider that you might need to create the **/var/backups/username** directory and that the directory should be owned by a user with the permissions **rwx------**. Also, each backup file should include the date of the backup in the filename and should be owned by a user with the permissions **rw-------**.

Modify the system **crontab** to run this command weekly.

_____

_____

_____

_____

_____

_____

_____

_____

_____

_____

_____

_____

_____

_____

_____

_____

_____

_____

_____

Chapter 17

Develop an Automation Security Policy

These labs should be performed on the Ubuntu operating system that you installed in Chapter 1, "Distributions and Key Components." Before you begin this lab, log in to the student account that you created during the installation process.

Lab 17.1 Securing *crontab* and *at*

Scenario: Based on the recommendations in *Linux Essentials for Cybersecurity*, make sure that the permissions on all **cron** and **at** files are as strict as possible.

Exception: If you change the permissions to **/var/spool/cron** and **/var/spool/at** on Ubuntu, regular users will not be able to use the corresponding commands (**crontab** and **at**). Change those permissions and test as the student user and then change the permission back to the original settings.

_____

_____

_____

_____

_____

_____

_____

_____

_____

_____

_____

_____

_____

_____

_____

_____

_____

_____

_____

_____

_____

Lab 17.2 Creating an Automation Security Policy

This lab does not have a specific correct answer. The goal is to use what you learned in Chapters 14, 15, and 16 of *Linux Essentials for Cybersecurity* to develop security policies for user and group accounts.

As a starting point, you can make use of some excellent sample security policies located at https://www.sans.org/security-resources/policies. Note that you may find some policies on this site very useful, as some are specific to accounts. While you can make use of some of the policies on this site and make use of the format of the policies, you should also include original work that you create, based on what you have learned in Chapters 14, 15, and 16 of *Linux Essentials for Cybersecurity*.

_____

_____

_____

_____

_____

_____

_____

_____

_____

_____

_____

_____

_____

_____

_____

_____

_____

_____

_____

_____

_____

_____

_____

_____

_____

_____

_____

_____

_____

Chapter 18

Networking Basics

These labs should be performed on the CentOS operating system that you installed in Chapter 1, "Distributions and Key Components." Before you begin this lab, log in to the student account that you created during the installation process.

Lab 18.1 Exploring Networking Components

Scenario 1: Understanding subnetting takes time and practice. Using the methods covered in the book, fill in the following tables.

Category	IP Address	Binary Format of IP Address
Address	75.99.120.100	
Netmask	28	
Network		
Broadcast		
First IP		
Last IP		
Maximum hosts in network		

Category	IP Address	Binary Format of IP Address
Address	144.77.66.40	
Netmask	18	
Network		
Broadcast		
First IP		
Last IP		
Maximum hosts in network		

Category	IP Address	Binary Format of IP Address
Address	196.40.70.10	
Netmask	26	
Network		
Broadcast		
First IP		
Last IP		
Maximum hosts in network		

Scenario 2: Think you have subnetting down? Try to get a high score on the subnetting game at https://www.subnetting.net/Start.aspx.

Scenario 3: Using the CentOS system, determine the standard ports for the following protocols. (The first one has been filled out for you.)

Protocol	Port
qotd	17/tcp
whois	
kerberos	
zserv	
syslog	
route	
nfs	

Chapter 19

Network Configuration

These labs should be performed on the CentOS and Ubuntu operating systems that you installed in Chapter 1, "Distributions and Key Components." The first lab (19.1) should be executed on the CentOS system, and the second lab (19.2) should be executed on the Ubuntu system. Before you begin this lab, log in to the student account that you created during the installation process.

Lab 19.1 Understanding Network Configuration on CentOS

To help you avoid accidentally breaking networking on your system, this lab focuses on viewing network information and not making permanent changes to network configuration.

STEP 1. Open a terminal window on your CentOS system.

STEP 2. Use the **ifconfig** command to display the current network configuration.

STEP 3. Use the **nmcli** command to determine whether the Network Manager is currently active.

STEP 4. Use the **arp** command to display the ARP table.

STEP 5. Use the **route** command to display the routing table.

STEP 6. Use the **route** command to add a new route for the 192.168.145.0/24 network, with gateway 192.168.0.199.

STEP 7. Use the **route** command to display the new routing table.

STEP 8. Display the current system name.

STEP 9. Change the current system name to **mymachine**.

STEP 10. Use the **host** command to perform a DNS query on ubuntu.com.

STEP 11. Use the **dig** command to perform a DNS query on ubuntu.com.

STEP 12. Use the **netstat** command to display TCP information.

STEP 13. Use the **netstat** command to display the routing table.

STEP 14. Use the **cat** command to display the contents of the file that contains the system's hostname.

STEP 15. Use the **cat** command to display the contents of the file that contains the hostname-to-IP-address translation.

_____

STEP 16. Use the **cat** command to display the contents of the file that contains the DNS servers for this system.

_____

STEP 17. Use the **cat** command to display the contents of the file that contains the setting that determines if networking should be turned on by default for this system.

_____

STEP 18. Use the **cat** command to display the contents of the file that contains the settings for the eth0 device (or emp0s3 if you are working on a virtual machine).

_____

_____

STEP 19. Reboot your system to revert all the networking settings back to the original.

_____

_____

Lab 19.2 Understanding Network Configuration on Ubuntu

To help you avoid accidentally breaking networking on your system, this lab focuses on viewing network information and not making permanent changes to network configuration.

STEP 1. Open a terminal window on your Ubuntu system.

_____

STEP 2. Use the correct **ip addr** command to display the current network configuration.

_____

_____

STEP 3. Use the correct **ip** command to display the routing table.

_____

STEP 4. Use the correct **ip** command to add a new route for the 192.168.145.0/24 network, with gateway 192.168.0.199.

_____

STEP 5. Use the correct **ip** command to display the new routing table.

_____

STEP 6. Use the **netstat** command to display UDP information.

_____

STEP 7. Use the **netstat** command to list network statistics.

_____

STEP 8. Use the **cat** command to display the contents of the file that contains NSS (Name Service Switch) configuration.

_____

STEP 9. Use the **cat** command to display the contents of the file that contains kernel parameters.

_____

STEP 10. Use the **cat** command to display the contents of the file that contains the persistent IP address settings.

_____

STEP 11. Use the **ping** command to determine if the ubuntu.com system is accessible via the network. (Send 10 ping requests only.)

_____

STEP 12. Use the **traceroute** command to display the routers that are used to connect to the ubuntu.com system.

_____

STEP 13. Reboot your system to revert all the networking settings back to the original.

_____

_____

Chapter 20

Network Service Configuration: Essential Services

These labs should be performed on the CentOS operating system that you installed in Chapter 1, "Distributions and Key Components." Before you begin these labs, log in to the student account that you created during the installation process.

Lab 20.1 Configuring a BIND Server

> **NOTE** Creating a full BIND server is beyond the scope of this book. In this lab you will create and explore the components of a caching-only server. A caching-only server should be used only by the local system.

STEP 1. Open a terminal window.

STEP 2. Switch to the root account by using the **su** command.

STEP 3. Run the **yum** command to install the **bind** and **bind-utils** software packages.

STEP 4. Edit the **/etc/named.conf** file to look as follows:

```
listen-on port 53 { 127.0.0.1; any; };
allow-query     { localhost; any; };
allow-query-cache      { localhost; any; };
```

STEP 5. Test the syntax of the **/etc/named.conf** file.

STEP 6. Restart the **named** service.

STEP 7. Check the status of the **named** service.

STEP 8. Enable the **named** service.

STEP 9. Execute the following commands to ensure that your firewall allows for DNS queries:

```
firewall-cmd --add-port=53/udp
firewall-cmd --add-port=53/udp --permanent
```

STEP 10. Test the service by executing the following command:

```
dig @localhost onecoursesource.com +trace
```

Lab 20.2 Configuring a Postfix Server

STEP 1.   Open a terminal window.

_____

STEP 2.   Switch to the root account by using the **su** command.

_____

STEP 3.   View the current value of the **inet_interfaces** setting for **Postconf**.

_____

STEP 4.   Change the value of the **inet_interfaces** setting to **all**.

_____

STEP 5.   Change the value of the **myhost** setting to **testserv**.

_____

STEP 6.   Create an email alias so email for the root user will be sent to the student user.

_____

STEP 7.   Execute the correct command to save the changes to the **/etc/alias** file to the Postfix database.

_____

Chapter 21

Network Service Configuration: Web Services

These labs should be performed on the CentOS operating system that you installed in Chapter 1, "Distributions and Key Components." Before you begin these labs, log in to the student account that you created during the installation process.

Lab 21.1 Configuring and Administering an Apache Server

Scenario: Install the **httpd** web server package and configure it as follows:

- Ensure that a test **index.html** page appears when you go to the main web server site (aka, **localhost**). This page should display the text **server up**.

- Change the log level to **info**.

- Limit the number of clients to 25.

- Use an **.htaccess** file to create a secured directory named **docs**.

- Create an Apache user named **student** that can access the **docs** directory.

_____

_____

_____

_____

_____

_____

_____

_____

_____

_____

_____

_____

_____

_____

_____

_____

_____

_____

_____

_____

_____

_____

_____

_____

Lab 21.2 Configuring a Proxy Server

Scenario: Configure your local system to act as a proxy server. By default, Squid is configured as a forward proxy server on port 3128. After installing Squid, start the service and use Firefox to test the proxy server.

Chapter 22

Connecting to Remote Systems

These labs should be performed on the CentOS operating system that you installed in Chapter 1, "Distributions and Key Components." Before you begin these labs, log in to the student account that you created during the installation process.

Lab 22.1 Configuring an FTP Server

Scenario: Install and configure a VSFTPD server for the local system that meets the following objectives:

- Disables anonymous FTP access
- Denies the bob user account access to the FTP server
- Limits the FTP server to two FTP client sessions
- Disables the ability for regular users to upload files via the FTP server

_____

_____

_____

_____

_____

_____

_____

_____

_____

_____

_____

_____

_____

_____

_____

_____

_____

_____

_____

_____

_____

_____

_____

Lab 22.2 Administering an SSH Server

Scenario: Configure the SSH server for the local system to meet the following objectives:

- Allow only Protocol 2 connections.
- Set the logging level to **VERBOSE**.
- Do not permit root logins.
- Deny the user bob the ability to log in via SSH.

Chapter 23

Develop a Network Security Policy

These labs should be performed on the CentOS operating system that you installed in Chapter 1, "Distributions and Key Components." Before you begin this lab, log in to the student account that you created during the installation process.

Lab 23.1 Administering Kernel Security Parameters

Scenario: Implement the following kernel parameter changes so they are persistent across reboots:

- Ignore all ping requests.
- Ignore all broadcast requests.
- Enable TCP SYN protection.
- Disable IP source routing.

_____

_____

_____

_____

_____

_____

_____

_____

_____

_____

Lab 23.2 Securing a System with TCP Wrappers

Scenario: Implement the following TCP Wrappers rules:

- Allow SSH connections from all hosts.
- Allow connections to the Very Security FTP server from hosts in your local network.
- Allow connections to the xinetd server for any clients that can be resolved via the hostname resolver tool.
- Block access to all other services that use TCP Wrappers from all systems.

_____

_____

_____

_____

_____

_____

_____

_____

_____

Lab 23.3 Configuring Network Time Protocol

Scenario: Configure your system to use the following NTP servers to configure the system time:

- 0.pool.ntp.org
- 1.pool.ntp.org
- 2.pool.ntp.org
- 3.pool.ntp.org

Lab 23.4 Creating a Networking Security Policy

This lab does not have a specific correct answer. The goal is to use what you learned in Chapters 19, 20, 21, and 22 of *Linux Essentials for Cybersecurity* to develop security policies for user and group accounts.

As a starting point, you can make use of some excellent sample security policies located at https://www.sans.org/security-resources/policies. Note that you may find some policies on this site very useful, as some are specific to accounts. While you can make use of some of the policies on this site and make use of the format of the policies, you should also include original work that you create, based on what you have learned in Chapters 19, 20, 21, and 22 of *Linux Essentials for Cybersecurity*.

Chapter 24

Process Control

These labs should be performed on the CentOS operating system that you installed in Chapter 1, "Distributions and Key Components." Before you begin this lab, log in to the student account that you created during the installation process.

Lab 24.1 Managing System Processes

STEP 1. Open a terminal window.

_____

STEP 2. List the processes that are running in the current shell.

_____

STEP 3. List all processes that are running on this system.

_____

STEP 4. Using the **grep** and **ps** commands, list all processes that are running on this system that end in *sh*.

_____

STEP 5. Using the **pgrep** command, list all processes that are running on this system that end in *sh*.

_____

STEP 6. Display all processes that are running by using the **top** command. (Keep this command running for the next few steps.)

_____

STEP 7. While in the **top** command, display the help screen.

_____

STEP 8. While in the **top** command, change the refresh period from 2 seconds to 5 seconds.

_____

STEP 9. Quit the **top** command.

_____

STEP 10. Execute the **gnome-calculator** program in the background.

_____

STEP 11. In the current shell, list all running jobs.

_____

STEP 12. Use the job number of the **gnome-calculator** program with the **kill** command to stop (kill) the program.

_____

STEP 13. Execute the **gnome-calculator** program in the background five times.

_____

_____

_____

_____

_____

STEP 14. Use the **killall** command to stop (kill) all instances of the **gnome-calculator** program.

_____

STEP 15. Execute the **gnome-calculator** program in the background.

_____

STEP 16. In the current shell, use the **ps** command to list all running processes.

_____

STEP 17. Change the process priority of the **gnome-calculator** program to a nice value of 15.

_____

_____

Lab 24.2 Displaying System Information

STEP 1. Open a terminal window.

_____

STEP 2. Execute the command that displays how long the system has been up and running.

_____

STEP 3. Execute the **uptime** command so the output is in "pretty" format.

_____

STEP 4. Execute the command that displays how much memory and swap space is available.

_____

STEP 5. Execute the **free** command so the output will be in megabytes.

_____

STEP 6. Execute the **free** command so the output will be updated every 2 seconds.

_____

STEP 7. Execute the **free** command so the output will display a total for each column.

_____

Chapter 25

System Logging

These labs should be performed on the CentOS operating system that you installed in Chapter 1, "Distributions and Key Components." Before you begin this lab, log in to the student account that you created during the installation process.

Lab 25.1 Managing Log Files

Scenario: Modify the CentOS system so the following log events take place:

- All **cron** messages of **debug** level only should be sent to the **/var/log/cron.debug** file.
- All messages from the **local3** service should be sent to the root user's terminal.

Verify that these changes have taken place correctly.

Lab 25.2 Configuring Log Rotation

Scenario: Modify the CentOS system so the following take place:

- By default, log files should be rotated daily.
- By default, a total of 10 backup copies of rotated log files should be kept.
- By default, log files that have been rotated should be compressed.
- All CUPS log files should be rotated weekly, and only 4 backup copies should be kept.

Chapter 26

Red Hat-Based Software Management

These labs should be performed on the CentOS operating system that you installed in Chapter 1, "Distributions and Key Components." Before you begin this lab, log in to the student account that you created during the installation process.

Lab 26.1 Managing Software Packages with *rpm*

STEP 1. Open a terminal window.

_____

STEP 2. List the contents of the directory that contains the RPM databases.

_____

STEP 3. Use the **rpm** command to list all RPMs that are currently installed on the system.

_____

STEP 4. Use the **rpm** command to list package information for the **gd** package.

_____

STEP 5. Use the **rpm** command to list all of the files that were installed with the **gd** package.

_____

STEP 6. Use the **rpm** command to list all of the configuration files that were installed with the **gd** package.

_____

STEP 7. Use the **rpm** command to list the package that provided the **/etc/cups/cupsd.conf** file.

_____

STEP 8. Use the **rpm** command to verify the package that provided the **/etc/cups/cupsd.conf** file.

_____

STEP 9. Use the **rpm** command to display the dependencies of the package that provided the **/etc/cups/cupsd.conf** file.

_____

Lab 26.2 Managing Software Packages with *yum*

STEP 1. Open a terminal window.

_____

STEP 2. List the contents of the directory that contains the yum repository configuration files.

_____

STEP 3. Use the **yum** command to determine if the **joe** package is currently installed on the system.

_____

STEP 4. Use the **yum** command to display information about the **joe** package.

_____

STEP 5. Use the **yum** command to install the **joe** package.

_____

STEP 6. Use the **yum** command to display standard software groups.

_____

STEP 7. Use the **yum** command to display all software groups.

_____

STEP 8. Use the **yum** command to uninstall the **joe** package.

_____

STEP 9. Use the **yum** command to display the currently used yum plugins.

_____

STEP 10. Use the **yum** command to display the available yum plugins.

_____

Chapter 27

Debian-Based Software Management

These labs should be performed on the Ubuntu operating system that you installed in Chapter 1, "Distributions and Key Components." Before you begin this lab, log in to the student account that you created during the installation process.

Lab 27.1 Managing Software Packages with *dpkg*

STEP 1. Open a terminal window.

STEP 2. Use the **dpkg** command to list all RPMs that are packages.

STEP 3. Use the **dpkg** command to list package information for the **acl** package.

STEP 4. Use the **dpkg** command to list all of the files that were installed with the **acl** package.

STEP 5. Use the **dpkg** command to list the package that provided the **/usr/bin/yes** file.

STEP 6. Use the **dpkg** command to verify the **acl** files.

Lab 27.2 Managing Software Packages with *apt*

STEP 1. Open a terminal window.

STEP 2. List the contents of the directory that contains the apt repository configuration files.

STEP 3. Use the **apt-cache** command to determine if there are any packages that include *joe* in the name or description.

STEP 4. Use the **apt** command to determine if the **joe** package is currently installed on the system.

STEP 5. Use the **apt** command to display package information about the **joe** package.

STEP 6. Use the **apt-cache** command to display dependency information about the **joe** package.

STEP 7. Use the **apt** command to install the **joe** package.

STEP 8. Use the **apt-get** command to completely uninstall the **joe** package.

Chapter 28

System Booting

These labs should be performed on the CentOS operating system that you installed in Chapter 1, "Distributions and Key Components." Before you begin these labs, log in to the student account that you created during the installation process.

Lab 28.1 Configuring GRUB Security

Scenario: You need to configure the current system so it is more secure because it will be located in a public area. Configure the GRUB boot so the following features are enabled:

- The GRUB menu should not appear. Instead, the default image should be automatically booted.
- Create a superuser GRUB account named **super** with the encrypted password **noaccess**.
- Create a regular GRUB account named **user** with the encrypted password **secured**.

Lab 28.2 Managing the Startup Process

This lab doesn't have a specific correct answer. The goal is to use what you learned in Chapter 28 of *Linux Essentials for Cybersecurity* to determine which services are unnecessary for your system. When you discover a service that you deem unnecessary, your next task is to change the boot process so this service will not be enabled at boot.

As you complete this lab, consider the following guidelines:

- Begin by listing all the services that are currently active for **multi-user.target**.
- Determine what each service provides (that is, which process it starts and what that process does).
- If you find an unnecessary process, disable it and then reboot your system.
- Record which services you disable so you know what to enable at a later date if something isn't working correctly.

Example: cups.service provides the CUPS (printer) server. This isn't needed on most servers, as no printing takes place.

Chapter 29

Develop a Software Management Security Policy

These labs should be performed on the CentOS operating system that you installed in Chapter 1, "Distributions and Key Components." Before you begin these labs, log in to the student account that you created during the installation process.

Lab 29.1 Exploring Common Vulnerabilities and Exposure Reports

Scenario: You have been asked to install the Apache web server on a system. Your company policy is to review recent CVEs before installing a new software product. View the three most recent CVEs for Apache and record the vulnerabilities for each.

_____

_____

_____

_____

_____

_____

_____

_____

_____

_____

_____

_____

_____

_____

_____

_____

_____

_____

_____

_____

_____

_____

_____

_____

_____

_____

_____

_____

Lab 29.2 Managing and Securing Legacy Services

Scenario: You have been asked to install a **tcpmux** server on the current system to be used with a legacy application from another system. Begin by installing the **xinetd** package. Then configure the **tcpmux** server, considering the following requirements:

- If there are more than 20 connection attempts per second, disable the service for 30 seconds.
- Permit only two active connections at a time.

Chapter 30

Footprinting

These labs should be performed on the CentOS operating system that you installed in Chapter 1, "Distributions and Key Components." Before you begin these labs, log in to the student account that you created during the installation process.

Lab 30.1 Using Probing Tools

STEP 1.   Open a terminal window.

_____

STEP 2.   Switch to the root account.

_____

STEP 3.   Execute the **nmap** command to probe for open TCP on the local system.

_____

STEP 4.   Execute the **nmap** command to probe for open UDP on the local system.

_____

STEP 5.   Execute the **nmap** command to probe for ports 5000–10000 on the local system.

_____

STEP 6.   Execute the **netstat** command to display a summary of network packet information by protocol.

_____

STEP 7.   Execute the **netstat** command to display the routing table.

_____

STEP 8.   Execute the **netstat** command to display all listening sockets.

_____

STEP 9.   Execute the **lsof** command to open network sockets.

_____

STEP 10. Execute the **lsof** command to open network sockets without resolving hostnames or port names.

_____

Lab 30.2 Scanning the Network

STEP 1.   Open a terminal window.

_____

STEP 2.   Switch to the root account.

_____

STEP 3.   Execute the **nmap** command for all systems in the 192.168.10.0 Class C network.

_____

STEP 4.   Execute the **tcpdump** command to capture 10 packets.

_____

STEP 5.   Execute the **tcpdump** command to capture 10 packets with full verbose data output.

_____

STEP 6.   Execute the **ifconfig** command to determine the name of your primary network interface.

_____

STEP 7.   Execute the **tcpdump** command to capture 10 packets specifically on the primary interface network.

_____

STEP 8.   Execute the **tcpdump** command to capture 10 packets for any SSH connection on the primary interface network.

_____

STEP 9.   Execute the **tcpdump** command to capture 500 packets. Save the output to the file named **/tmp/tcpdump.data**.

_____

STEP 10. Execute the **tcpdump** command to view the contents of the **/tmp/tcpdump.data** file.

_____

Chapter 31

Firewalls

This lab should be performed on the CentOS operating system that you installed in Chapter 1, "Distributions and Key Components." Before you begin this lab, log in to the student account that you created during the installation process.

Lab 31.1 Creating a Firewall to Protect a System

Scenario: Using the **iptables** command, create a firewall for the local system that meets the following objectives:

- Allows incoming connections for the SSH and FTP ports from any system
- Allows incoming connections for the telnet port for any system in the 192.168.1.0/24 network
- Logs all other incoming connections
- Drops all other incoming connections by changing the default policy

NOTE Do not save the changes you make during this lab exercise.

Chapter 32

Intrusion Detection

This lab should be performed on the CentOS operating system that you installed in Chapter 1, "Distributions and Key Components." Before you begin this lab, log in to the student account that you created during the installation process.

Lab 32.1 Creating an Intrusion Detection Security Plan

This lab doesn't have a specific correct answer. The goal is to use what you learned in Chapter 32 of *Linux Essentials for Cybersecurity* to develop security policies for intrusion detection.

As a starting point, you can make use of some excellent sample security policies available at https://www.sans.org/security-resources/policies. You may find some policies at this site very useful, as some are specific to accounts. For example, there is a sample policy called Disaster Recovery Plan Policy. While you can make use of some of the policies on this site and make use of the format of the policies, you should also include original work that you create, based on what you have learned in Chapters 9, 10, 11, and 12 of *Linux Essentials for Cybersecurity.*

_____

_____

_____

_____

_____

_____

_____

_____

_____

_____

_____

_____

_____

_____

_____

_____

_____

_____

_____

_____

_____

_____

_____

_____

_____

_____

_____

_____

Chapter 33

Additional Security Tasks

These labs should be performed on the CentOS operating system that you installed in Chapter 1, "Distributions and Key Components." Before you begin these labs, log in to the student account that you created during the installation process.

Lab 33.1 Configuring *fail2ban*

Scenario: Install the **fail2ban** software and configure it, keeping in mind the following requirements:

- Set the ban length to 5 minutes.
- Set the number of failures to 10.
- Set the **findtime** setting to 10 minutes.
- Make sure the service is enabled.

Lab 33.2 Encrypting Files with *gpg*

STEP 1. Open a terminal window.

_____

STEP 2. Create **gpg** keys using RSA and RSA encryption. Use **Joe User** for the Real Name, **joe@ user.com** for the email address, and default values at all the other prompts.

_____

STEP 3. Create a public key file named **testkey** for Joe User.

_____

STEP 4. Import the **testkey** public key into the GPG database.

_____

STEP 5. Copy the **/etc/hosts** file to your home directory.

_____

STEP 6. Copy the **/etc/hosts** file to your home directory.

_____

STEP 7. Encrypt the **hosts** file that is in your home directory using the public key that you created in step 2.

_____

CISCO

Connect, Engage, Collaborate

The Award Winning Cisco Support Community

Attend and Participate in Events

Ask the Experts
Live Webcasts

Knowledge Sharing

Documents
Blogs
Videos

Top Contributor Programs

Cisco Designated VIP
Hall of Fame
Spotlight Awards

Multi-Language Support

https://supportforums.cisco.com